BY THE NUMBERS

SKYBOX PRESS

MIKE "MURPH" MURPHY

I go back with the San Francisco Giants as far as anyone can go. In 1958, when the Giants played at Seals Stadium in their first season out west, I got a job as the visiting team's batboy. I was 16. I've been with the team ever since, moving up to assistant clubhouse manager—back when the uniforms were all wool and had to be sent out to the cleaners—and then, in 1980, to clubhouse manager, my job for 34 years. Now I serve as senior advisor. One of my many tasks over the years has been doling out uniform numbers.

There was never any physical list of available numbers; I just kept them in my head. We'll let a guy pick whatever number he wants. But if a player is just making it to the big leagues, we'll just give him a number. Then, usually, he'll just stick with that number wherever he goes. Like George Kontos: He was 70 with the Yankees, so when he got traded here in 2012, he wanted 70.

I've always tried to accommodate the players' needs and desires—I want them all to feel comfortable in a Giants uniform. Sometimes, young guys don't know the team history, and they'll ask for a number they can't have. We had this one kid—I can't remember his name, but he wanted 25, and I told him, "You can't have it." That was right after Barry Bonds retired from the Giants.

Usually, the guys who are fan favorites, like Robbie Nen, Will Clark, those kind of guys, I hold back their numbers for at least a year and won't give them out right away. Another number we haven't given out is 55. That is still Timmy's number.

When Willie McCovey left for a few years back in the '70s, I kept 44 for him, but no one ever asked for it. Maybe they knew better, but back then everyone wanted low numbers. Now, the younger generation, they want higher numbers on their back. But no one has asked for a three-digit number—at least, not yet!

When new players join the team and they want a number that somebody already has, the cost to get a guy to switch seems to be an expensive watch—just ask Bruce Bochy*.

I play the lottery using uniform numbers of different managers. I usually always pick 1 for Alvin Dark, 3 for Herman Franks, and 12 for Jim Davenport, and then I mix it up for the other number, sometimes picking 15 for Bochy, 20 for Frank Robinson, 23 for Felipe Alou, 33 for Roger Craig.

I haven't hit the jackpot yet, but after 60 years working with the San Francisco Giants, it sure feels like I won the lottery.

There are 24 palm trees in Willie Mays Plaza
in honor of the Say Hey Kid

WILLIE MAYS

The first uniform number I remember wearing was 0, when I was with the Birmingham Black Barons of the Negro American League. That was in 1948. I was 17 years old. You don't get much choice as a kid; you take what you get. Same thing for my minor league teams: in Trenton, NJ, I wore number 12 because that was the uniform they gave me, and it fit. Later, with the Triple-A Minneapolis Millers, I wore number 28. No reason other than that's what I got.

I played my first Major League game with the New York Giants on May 25, 1951. I first was given number 14. An outfielder named Jack McGuire had number 24. It wasn't that I wanted 24, but I didn't like 14. At that time, outfielders wore higher numbers, numbers in the twenties, not numbers in the teens. So 14, it just didn't feel right to me.

Lucky for me, the Giants made a roster change just three days after my debut. Jack McGuire was selected off waivers by the Pittsburgh Pirates on May 28, 1951. He moved on, and I got number 24, and that suited me fine.

In 1952, I was drafted into the Army. I was in the service for 22 months, and missed most of the 1952 season, as well as all of 1953. I was stationed at Ft. Eustis, Virginia. Since I also played ball there, the Giants sent uniforms with Ft. Eustis on the front, and 24 on the back.

While I was in the service, a pitcher named Mario Picone appeared in a couple of games for the Giants and wore number 24. That was at the end of 1952. When I returned to New York in 1954, number 24 was waiting for me. After Picone, no other Giant wore 24, or even asked for the number; it was mine. Everybody knew the situation after that.

I played my last game 45 years ago, and still I hear from young players who tell me they wear 24 because of me. Recently, this one kid who was pitching in Chattanooga, Tennessee, told me he knew that I'd started my pro career there. During the summer of 1947, while I was still in high school, I played with the Chattanooga Choo-Choos of the Negro Southern League. That kid knew about that, and he knew all the ballparks I had played in back then.

I'm touched that so many people think of me when they see the number 24. When I see Giants fans nowadays wearing their jerseys with my number on the back, it brings back so many memories, and it makes me feel young again!

BARRY BONDS

My father, Bobby Bonds, wore number 25 during his seven years as a Giant, but all through high school and college, I wore number 24 because I was born on July 24. It also happened to be my godfather Willie Mays' number as well.

When I came up to the big leagues with the Pirates in 1986, both of those numbers were already taken: 24 by an infielder named Denny González, and 25 by pitcher José DeLeón. The Pirates gave me number 7. People made a thing about "Bonds 7," like "James Bond 007," but when Denny González was sent down to the minors, I got number 24 back.

When I signed with the Giants after the 1992 season, I would've loved to have worn number 24— and Willie actually offered it to me. I was so honored that he wanted to give that to me, but because it was retired, Major League Baseball wouldn't allow it. Willie Mays is the greatest and was my idol growing up.

Giants managing partner Peter McGowan suggested that I wear number 25, the same number as my dad. Getting to wear the same uniform with the same

number as my dad was special in a way that words can't describe. San Francisco is home, and although it sounds clichéd, it truly was my dream come true to come back and play on the same team as my dad and my godfather.

I'm both honored and humbled that the Giants are retiring my number. As I've always said, the Giants and Giants fans are a part of my family. Growing up, Candlestick Park was my home away from home. It was where my dad and godfather Willie played, and for me to have played on the same field as them, wear the same uniform, and now have my number retired along with Willie and the other Giants legends, it is extremely special.

Number 25 has meant a lot to me throughout my career, and it is even more special that I got to share that with my dad.

JUAN MARICHAL

Many aspects of my Major League Baseball career were nods to my Dominican roots. I became a pitcher because of Bombo Ramos, who was a star pitcher for the Dominican Republic national team when I was a kid. I had been a shortstop, but after I saw Bombo pitch, I decided I wanted to be a pitcher, too. I tried to imitate him in every way.

I wore 14 when I pitched for the United Fruit Company, and then I wore 20 when I played for the Dominican Air Force team. Those were just the numbers I was given. But when I joined the Giants in 1960, I got to choose my number. I picked number 27, because February 27 is Dominican Republic Independence Day. Wearing that number paid homage to my country.

I never thought about changing my number, and no one ever asked me to switch during all my years with the Giants. But I ended up wearing 27 only with the Giants. When I got to Boston in 1974, Carlton Fisk, the great Red Sox catcher, already had number 27. I wore 21, and I liked it because it was Roberto Clemente's number.

A lot of Dominican players have chosen to wear number 27. Vladimir Guerrero wore 27 during his Hall of Fame career, and Big Papi, David Ortiz, wore 27 during his first six seasons. Also, pitcher Jose Rijo was an All-Star and a World Series champion and World Series MVP wearing number 27.

I feel great pride having had my number retired by the Giants. It is special to me personally, and I feel it is a tribute to my beloved Dominican Republic.

ORLANDO CEPEDA

In the early 1950s, Willie Mays came to Puerto Rico to play winter ball. I was a teenager. I remember I said to my mother, "I want to be a professional ballplayer like Willie Mays."

My father, Pedro, played professional baseball. He played in Puerto Rico, Cuba, Venezuela, and the Dominican Republic. He wore number 30, so when I got to the big leagues in 1958, I requested number 30 to honor my father.

During my ninth season with the Giants, I was traded to the Cardinals. Number 30 was already taken, so I wore 28, but after the season, the player who had number 30 left, so I got it back. The same thing happened with the Braves: I started out wearing number 20, and then, when number 30 came available, I got it back. Later in my career, I wore number 12 with the Athletics and number 25 with the Red Sox because 30 was already taken.

In 1974, I did not play the first part of the year, but then, in early August, the Royals signed me as a free agent the day after they made a deal with the Cardinals for an outfielder named Richie Scheinblum, who wore number 30, so I was able to wear my number 30 to finish my career.

I love that number 30. My father died the day before I played my first game in the minor leagues, so he never got to see me as a professional ballplayer. When the Giants told me they were going to retire my number, it was a huge compliment. It means a lot to me that number 30 is going to be there forever. It is an honor not only for me, but also for my father, and I am very proud of that.

GAYLORD PERRY

When I played in the minors, I wore different numbers—whatever they had. It didn't matter. Coming up, you were just glad to get a number. I remember at AAA in Tacoma, we would get the previous year's uniforms from the big league club. One year, I got Willie McCovey's old uniform, number 44.

I made it to the Majors in 1962. That year I split time between San Francisco and Tacoma, and at different times I wore number 22 and number 28. I didn't ask for those; they were given to me by the clubhouse manager, Eddie Logan. I didn't ask questions. I just said, "Thank you."

I got number 36 when I came up for good in 1963, and it stuck. After the 1971 season, I got traded to the Indians, and I wore number 36 there. When I was 36 years old, Cleveland traded me to the Rangers, and I got number 36 there. Later, I wore 36 with the Padres, then with the Yankees, and then, before the 1981 season, I signed as a free agent with the Braves.

When I went to Spring Training with Atlanta, former Giants outfielder Gary Matthews already had number 36. I told him, "Before Spring Training is over, I'm going to have my number." Sure enough, Gary got traded to the Phillies right before Opening Day, and I got my number 36.

I wore 36 when I joined the Mariners, and 36 was the number on my uniform with the Royals when I finally hung it up in 1983. I was 45 years old.

I'm very thankful and happy the Giants retired my number. Still today, I always sign my name with "#36."

WILLIE MCCOVEY

As a young ballplayer, I idolized Hank Aaron. I grew up in the same town as Hank—Mobile, Alabama. He wore number 44, and when I got called up in the summer of 1959, nobody was wearing 44, so I asked for that. [The last Giant to wear 44 before Willie McCovey was pitcher Don Johnson, who played part of one season with San Francisco in 1958.]

I never had to wear another number in my career, even when I played for other teams. When I joined the Padres in 1974, Vicente Romo had 44. When he was asked to let me have it, he said, "Who's he?" He really hated to give it up, but he gave in and took 45 and let me have 44.

Then, when I went to the A's toward the end of the 1976 season, number 44 was available, surprisingly, because no one had ever worn number 44 in the team's history.

I came back to the Giants in 1977, and I found that Murph had kept 44 in mothballs for me. I don't know if any other players had asked for it while I was away, but nobody got it.

I played my last four seasons in San Francisco wearing 44, and shortly after I retired in September 1980, the Giants retired my number.

I remember the ceremony on the field at Candlestick Park. It was quite a day and quite an honor. It's a special moment when your team recognizes you that way and you realize that no one will ever wear your number again.

15 16 BRUCE BOCHY

I started wearing number 15 when I signed as a free agent with San Diego in 1983. I wore it for the last five years of my career as a player with the Padres, I kept it when I managed the team for 12 seasons from 1995 to 2006, and I chose number 15 when I took over as manager of the Giants in 2007.

In 2011, we acquired Carlos Beltran at the trade deadline. He had worn number 15 for more than a decade with the Royals, the Astros, and the Mets. Our general manager, Brian Sabean, let me know that Carlos really wanted to wear number 15. I said Carlos could have it, and I switched to number 16. I wanted him to be comfortable. I told Carlos I did not want anything in return, but he went ahead and bought me a beautiful Panerai wristwatch.

Carlos wound up playing with us for just a couple of months, and then, in the off-season, he signed with the Cardinals. I got number 15 back, and a fancy watch, which just goes to show that timing is everything.

42
45
46

KIRK RUETER

I wore number 42 when I came up with the Expos, and I stuck with it when I was traded to the Giants. Then, in 1997, Major League Baseball decided to retire 42 league-wide in honor of Jackie Robinson. Players who were wearing 42 could keep it—Mariano Rivera did—but for me, it seemed a no-brainer to give it up. Murph suggested 45, and I took it. A few weeks later, we traded for Terry Mulholland, who had worn 45 in two previous stints with the Giants. Terry asked me if he could have number 45, and since it was new to me, I said O.K. I didn't get a Rolex or anything; I just let him have it, then I went back to Murph and said, "What else have you got?" No one was wearing 46, so I took that and kept 46 for the rest of my career.

26
20
00

JEFFREY LEONARD

I had been wearing number 30 with the Astros, but Chili Davis had it when I was traded to the Giants in 1981. I was given number 26, and I was fine with that, but two years later, I'd had so many injuries that I wanted a fresh start. I asked for 00, but the general manager, Al Rosen—who had traded me to San Francisco when he was running the Astros—thought that if I wore 00, it would give the media ammo to use against me if I ever had a drought at the plate. Instead, I chose to wear 20 in honor of Frank Robinson, who was the manager when I joined the Giants and had recently been let go.

After two years wearing 20, I went back and said I wanted number 00. And it worked, as I was named an All-Star for the first time in my 11th season in the big leagues. No other Giant has ever worn 00, which is nice, because it's unique and fans remember me for that.

8
19

KEVIN FRANDSEN

Dave Righetti grew up with my dad in San Jose, and our families were close. Dave often visited my brother, DJ, in the hospital when DJ was battling cancer. My brother's favorite number was 19 because of Dave, who had won Rookie of the Year, was an All-Star twice, and pitched a no-hitter wearing number 19 for the Yankees. Dave wore 19 when he pitched for the Giants from 1991 to 1993, and he wore it when he he became the pitching coach in 2000.

In 2004, I was drafted by the Giants and sent to the A-league Salem-Keizer Volcanoes in Oregon. By sheer coincidence, a uniform with the number 19 was hanging in my locker. That seemed like a good omen, and my first phone call was to DJ. My brother died later that year—he was 19.

Two years later, I got called up to the big leagues. I initially wore number 8, but then, one day, we got home from a road trip and I was stunned to see, hanging in my locker, a San Francisco Giants uniform with my name and number 19 on the back. I never asked for that; it was all Dave's idea. That simple but significant gesture tells you everything you need to know about what kind of person Dave Righetti is.

28

BUSTER POSEY

I was given number 28 my first Spring Training. I wore 8 in college, but 28 was what I was given, and I was happy to get it.

WHY I WEAR NUMBER

1

GREGOR BLANCO

I've always loved number 1. It was one of my first numbers in the big leagues. I think it really speaks to the type of player I am. You always know number 1 is fast and plays hard.

50

TY BLACH

Number 50 was hanging in my locker when I came up. It's working for me.

WHY I WEAR NUMBER

7

GORKYS HERNANDEZ

My birthday is on the seventh, and 7 was my first number as a pro in the minors. It was also my number in winter ball in Venezuela.

40

MADISON BUMGARNER

I am not superstitious. When I got called up, they gave me number 40, and I liked the way it looked.

WHY I WEAR NUMBER

5

NICK HUNDLEY

I wore 4 and 40 with the Padres, the Orioles, and the Rockies, but when I joined the Giants, 4 was retired and Madison Bumgarner has 40, so I took 5. I like the single digit.

26

CORY GEARRIN

Both my parents played sports in college and wore number 13, so I put the two together and wear 26.

WHY I WEAR NUMBER

9

BRANDON BELT

When you are a rookie, you don't ask questions. I got number 9 and was happy to have it. I've never been asked to give it up, but I'd be open—if the price is right.

35

BRANDON CRAWFORD

I was told that I was given number 35 because it had been worn by a couple of great homegrown shortstops, Chris Speier and Rich Aurilia.

WHY I WEAR NUMBER

29

JEFF SAMARDZIJA

I like 29 because John Smoltz wore it. Surprisingly, it's been available with all four teams I've played with. I've never had to buy a guy a watch to get it.

60

HUNTER STRICKLAND

When I got called up in 2014, I was issued number 60. We won the World Series that year, so I am sticking with it.

WHY I WEAR NUMBER

10

EVAN LONGORIA

I was number 3 my entire career, but when I was traded to the Giants, I learned it was retired. I like low numbers, and 10 pays homage to my having played 10 years in the Majors.

12

JOE PANIK

I'm from New York, and Wade Boggs wore 12 with the Yankees, so I wore 12 in Little League. When I made it to the big leagues, it was complete luck of the draw that 12 was hanging in my locker.

WHY I WEAR NUMBER

8

HUNTER PENCE

As a kid, I always wore number 8. It wasn't available when I played with the Astros and the Phillies, but I got it back when I became a Giant.

28

34

CHRIS STRATTON

I was given number 68 last season. This year,
I wanted a new number and got 34.

WHY I WEAR NUMBER

22

ANDREW MCCUTCHEN

Growing up, I wore 24 for Ken Griffey Jr., but when I came
up with the Pirates, a pitcher named Tom Gorzelanny had
it—what pitcher wears number 24? So I wore 22, and I
made a name for myself with it, so I stayed with it.

ALL-TIME UNIFORM NUMBERS
NUMERICAL ORDER

NAME	POSITION	SEASONS
0		
Al Oliver	IF	1984
00		
Jeffrey Leonard	OF	1987-1988
1		
Bill Posedel	Coach	1959-1960
Alvin Dark	Manager	1961-1964
Randy Hundley	C	1965
Bob Barton	C	1966-1969
John McNamara	Coach	1971-1973
Ozzie Virgil	Coach	1974-1975
Craig Robinson	IF	1975-1976
Marty Perez	IF	1977
Dave Bristol	Coach	1978-1979
Jim Davenport	Coach	1979-1983
Dave Bristol	Manager	1980
Jesus Figueroa	OF	1981
Jim Wohlford	OF	1982
Danny Ozark	Coach	1984
Jim Davenport	Manager	1985
Mike Aldrete	OF	1986
Don Zimmer	Coach	1987
Tony Perezchica	IF	1988
Ernest Riles	OF	1989-1990
Mark Leonard	OF	1990-1992, 1994
Dave Martinez	OF	1994
Glenallen Hill	OF	1995-1996
Wilson Delgado	IF	1998
Alex Diaz	OF	1998
Armando Rios	OF	1998-2001
Cody Ransom	IF	2001
Kenny Lofton	OF	2002
Neifi Perez	IF	2003
Damon Minor	IF	2004
Angel Chavez	IF	2005
Adam Shabala	OF	2005
Travis Ishikawa	IF	2006
Bengie Molina	C	2007-2010
Jose Guillen	OF	2010
Tim Flannery	Coach	2010-2014
Ehire Adrianza	IF	2015-2016
Ramiro Pena	IF	2016
Jae-gyun Hwang	IF	2017
Gregor Blanco	OF	2018

NAME	POSITION	SEASONS
2		
Salty Parker	Coach	1958-1961
Joe Pignatano	C	1962
Jim Coker	C	1963
Jack Hiatt	C	1965-1966
Dick Dietz	C	1966-1972
Marc Hill	C	1975-1980
Joe Pettini	IF	1980-1983
Chuck Hiller	Coach	1985
Luis Quinones	IF	1986
Chris Speier	IF	1987
Brett Butler	OF	1988-1990
Darren Lewis	OF	1991-1995
Mark Leonard	OF	1995
Mel Hall	OF	1996
Rick Wilkins	C	1997
Doug Mirabelli	C	1998
Chris Jones	OF	1998
Edwards Guzman	C/IF	1999
Wayne Gomes	P	2001
Cody Ransom	IF	2002-2004
Brian Dallimore	IF	2005
Randy Winn	OF	2005-2009
Emmanuel Burriss	IF	2010-2012
Juan Perez	IF	2013-2015
Denard Span	OF	2016-2017

3

Retired in 1983 in honor of
Bill Terry, IF, N.Y. Giants, 1923-1936

NAME	POSITION	SEASONS
Herman Franks	Coach	1958
Hobie Landrith	C	1959
Wes Westrum	Coach	1960-1961
Whitey Lockman	Coach	1962-1964
Herman Franks	Manager	1965-1968
Ozzie Virgil	Coach	1969-1972
Mike Sadek	C	1973, 1975-1981
Jeff Ransom	C	1981-1982
Danny Ozark	Coach	1983

4

Retired in 1984 in honor of
Mel Ott, OF, N.Y. Giants, 1926-1947

5

NAME	POSITION	SEASONS
Hobie Landrith	C	1960-1961
Wes Westrum	Coach	1969
John Stephenson	C	1970
Joe Amalfitano	Coach	1972-1975

NAME	POSITION	SEASONS
Bobby Winkles	Coach	1976-1977
Dave Bristol	Coach	1978
Jim Lefebvre	Coach	1980-1982
Wallace Johnson	IF	1983
John Rabb	C	1983-1984
Bob Lillis	Coach	1986-1996
Darryl Hamilton	OF	1997-1998
Robby Thompson	Coach	2000-2001
Tsuyoshi Shinjo	OF	2002
Ray Durham	IF	2003-2008
Travis Ishikawa	IF	2008
Juan Uribe	IF	2009-2010
Pat Burrell	OF	2011
Ryan Theriot	IF	2012
Joe Lefebvre	Coach	2013-2015
Matt Duffy	IF	2015-2016
Nick Hundley	C	2017-2018
6		
Bob Schmidt	C	1958
Hank Sauer	OF	1958-1959
Neil Wilson	P	1960
Wes Westrum	Coach	1961
Ed Bailey	C	1961-1963
Herman Franks	Coach	1964
Dick Bertell	C	1965-1966
Harry "Peanuts" Lowery	Coach	1967-1968
Dave Rader	C	1971
Fran Healy	C	1972
Ken Rudolph	C	1974
Joe Altobelli	Manager	1977-1979
Rennie Stennett	IF	1980-1981
Champ Summers	OF	1982-1983
Don Buford	Coach	1984
Rocky Bridges	Coach	1985
Robby Thompson	IF	1986-1996
J.T. Snow	IF	1997-2005
Tim Flannery	Coach	2007-2010
Jose Guillen	OF	2010
Orlando Cabrera	IF	2011
Brett Pill	IF	2011-2013
Ehire Adrianza	IF	2014
Marlon Byrd	OF	2015
Jarrett Parker	OF	2016-2017
7		
Valmy Thomas	C	1958
Jose Pagan	IF	1959
Dale Long	OF	1960

Eddie Fisher	P	1960
Harvey Kuenn	OF	1961-1965
Len Gabrielson	OF	1965-1966
Norm Siebern	IF	1967
Jack Hiatt	C	1967-1969
Charlie Fox	Manager	1970-1974
Hank Sauer	Coach	1979
Milt May	C	1980-1983
Steve Nicosia	C	1983-1984
Atlee Hammaker	P	1985
Bob Melvin	C	1986-1988
Kevin Mitchell	OF	1989-1991
John Patterson	OF	1992-1995
Marvin Benard	OF	1995-2003
Pedro Feliz	IF	2004-2007
Emmanuel Burriss	IF	2008-2009
Mark DeRosa	OF	2010-2011
Gregor Blanco	OF	2012-2016
Aaron Hill	IF	2017
Gorkys Hernandez	OF	2018

8

Roger McCardell	C	1959
Harry "Cookie" Lavagetto	Coach	1964-1967
Andy Gilbert	Coach	1973-1975
Bob Rodgers	Coach	1976
Tom Haller	Coach	1977-1978
Larry Shepard	Coach	1979
Vern Benson	Coach	1980
Joe Morgan	IF	1981-1982
Joel Youngblood	OF	1983-1988
Ed Jurak	IF	1989
Gary Carter	C	1990
Kirt Manwaring	C	1991-1996
Desi Wilson	IF	1996
Damon Berryhill	C	1997
Shawon Dunston	IF	1998
Calvin Murray	OF	1999-2002
Tom Goodwin	OF	2002
Yorvit Torrealba	C	2003-2005
Yamid Haad	C	2005
Kevin Frandsen	IF	2006
Shea Hillenbrand	IF	2006
Scott McClain	IF	2007
Eugenio Velez	IF	2008-2010
Jeff Keppinger	IF	2011
Hunter Pence	OF	2012-2018

9

Wes Westrum	Coach	1958-1959
Bob Schmidt	C	1960-1961
Wes Westrum	Coach	1962-1963
Del Crandall	C	1964
Charlie Fox	Coach	1965-1968
John Harrell	C	1969
Wes Westrum	Coach	1970-1971

Wes Westrum	Manager	1974-1975
Jim Davenport	Coach	1976-1978
Hector "Heity" Cruz	OF	1979
Jim Wohlford	OF	1980-1981
Don Buford	Coach	1982-1983
Manny Trillo	IF	1984-1985
Rick Lancellotti	OF	1986
Randy Kutcher	OF	1986-1987
Rob Wilfong	IF	1987
Ivan DeJesus	IF	1987
Kevin Mitchell	OF	1988
Matt Williams	IF	1989-1996
Brent Mayne	C	1998-1999
Scott Servais	C	2000
Edwards Guzman	C	2001
Yorvit Torrealba	C	2001-2002
Marquis Grissom	OF	2003-2005
Mark Sweeney	IF	2006-2007
Carney Lansford	Coach	2008-2009
Pat Burrell	OF	2010
Brandon Belt	IF	2011-2018

10

Ray Jablonski	IF	1958
Jose Pagan	IF	1959
Don Blasingame	IF	1960-1961
Jose Cardenal	OF	1963-1964
Masanori Murakami	P	1964-1965
Bob Schroder	IF	1965-1968
John Stephenson	C	1969
Al Gallagher	IF	1970-1973
Mike Phillips	IF	1974-1975
Johnnie LeMaster	IF	1975-1985
Ron Roenicke	OF	1985
Brad Gulden	C	1986
Mackey Sasser	C	1987
Matt Williams	IF	1987-1988
Ken Oberkfell	IF	1989
Dave Anderson	IF	1990-1991
Royce Clayton	IF	1991-1995
David McCarty	IF/OF	1995-1996
Jose Vizcaino	IF	1997
Ron Wotus	Coach	1998-2003
Neifi Perez	IF	2004
Deivi Cruz	IF	2004
Ron Wotus	Coach	2005
Jose Vizcaino	IF	2006
Tomas De la Rosa	IF	2006
Dave Roberts	OF	2007-2008
Travis Ishikawa	IF	2009-2010
Miguel Tejada	IF	2011
Tony Abreu	IF	2013-2014
Chris Dominguez	IF	2014
Tyler Colvin	OF	2014
Eduardo Nunez	IF	2016-2017
Evan Longoria	IF	2018

11

12

Jim Davenport	IF	1958-1970
Gary Thomasson	OF	1972-1977
Jim Davenport	Coach	1979-1983
Dusty Baker	OF	1984
Phil Ouellette	C	1986
Eddie Milner	OF	1987
Dusty Baker	Coach	1988-1992
Dusty Baker	Manager	1993-2002
Jeffrey Hammonds	OF	2004
Edgardo Alfonzo	IF	2005
Steve Finley	OF	2006
Nate Schierholtz	OF	2007
Jose Castillo	IF	2008
Nate Schierholtz	OF	2008-2012
Xavier Nady	OF	2012
Guillermo Quiroz	C	2013
Johnny Monell	C	2013
Joe Panik	IF	2014-2018

13

Mark Davis	P	1983-1987
Ernie Camacho	P	1989-1990
J.R. Phillips	IF	1994-1995
Charlie Hayes	IF	1998-1999
Edwards Guzman	C/IF	2001
Edgardo Alfonzo	IF	2003-2004
Omar Vizquel	IF	2005-2008
Jesus Guzman	IF	2009
Cody Ross	OF	2010-2011
Joaquin Arias	IF	2012-2015
Mike Leake	P	2015
Ehire Adrianza	IF	2016
Will Smith	P	2016, 2018

14

Don Taussig	OF	1958
Joe Amalfitano	IF	1960-1961
Dick Phillips	IF	1962
Jesus Alou	OF	1963-1968
George Foster	OF	1969-1971
Frank Duffy	IF	1971
Dave Rader	C	1972-1976
Gary Alexander	C	1976-1977
Phil Nastu	P	1978
Vida Blue	P	1978-1981
Reggie Smith	IF	1982
Ron Pruitt	C	1982-1983
Atlee Hammaker	P	1984-1990
Vida Blue	P	1985-1986
Mark Dewey	P	1990
Mike Remlinger	P	1991
Chris James	OF	1992

Todd Benzinger	IF	1993-1994
Shawn Barton	P	1995-1996
Trenidad Hubbard	C	1996
Mark Lewis	IF	1997
Rey Sanchez	IF	1998
F.P. Santangelo	IF/OF	1999
Terrell Lowery	OF	2000
Andres Gallaraga	IF	2001
Ryan Vogelsong	P	2001
Tony Torcato	OF	2002
Andres Gallaraga	IF	2003
Brian Dallimore	IF	2004
Jeff Fassero	P	2005-2006
Chad Santos	IF	2006
Fred Lewis	OF	2006-2010
Mike Fontenot	IF	2010-2011
Francisco Peguero	OF	2012-2013
Guillermo Quiroz	C	2014
Brandon Hicks	IF	2014
Jackson Williams	C	2015
Casey McGehee	IF	2015
Trevor Brown	C	2016

15

Andre Rodgers	IF	1958-1959
Jose Pagan	IF	1960-1965
Dick Schofield	IF	1965-1966
Ken Henderson	OF	1967-1972
Jack Clark	OF	1975
Chris Arnold	IF	1975-1976
Mike Ivie	OF	1978-1981
Bob Brenly	C	1981-1988
Terry Kennedy	C	1989
Greg Litton	IF	1990-1991
Bob Brenly	Coach	1992-1996
Jim Davenport	Coach	1996
Sonny Jackson	Coach	1997-1999
Doug Mirabelli	C	2000
Ryan Jensen	P	2001
Sonny Jackson	Coach	2002
Gene Glynn	Coach	2003-2006
Bruce Bochy	Manager	2007-2011
Carlos Beltran	OF	2011
Bruce Bochy	Manager	2012-2018

16

Ed Bressoud	IF	1958-1961
Norm Larker	IF	1963
Jim Ray Hart	IF	1963-1973
Steve Ontiveros	IF	1973-1976
Randy Elliott	OF	1977
Roger Metzger	IF	1978-1980
Jeff Ransom	C	1981
Dave Bergman	IF	1981-1983
Fran Mullins	IF	1984
Harry Spilman	IF	1986-1988
Tony Perezchica	IF	1988

Terry Kennedy	C	1990-1991
Carlos Alfonso	Coach	1992
Bobby Bonds	Coach	1993-1996
Ron Perranoski	Coach	1997-1999
Sonny Jackson	Coach	2000-2001
Reggie Sanders	OF	2002
Jeffrey Hammonds	OF	2003
Ron Wotus	Coach	2004
Joe Lefebvre	Coach	2005-2007
Emmanuel Burriss	IF	2008
Pat Misch	P	2008
Edgar Renteria	IF	2009-2010
Bruce Bochy	Manager	2011
Angel Pagan	OF	2012-2016
Phil Nevin	Coach	2017
Austin Jackson	OF	2018

17

Jim Finigan	IF	1958
Andre Rodgers	IF	1960
Charles "Cap" Peterson	IF/OF	1962-1966
Cesar Gutierrez	IF	1967
Bob Etheridge	IF	1969*
Bob Heise	IF	1970-1971
Chris Arnold	IF	1973-1974
Randy Moffitt	P	1975-1981
Bob Tufts	P	1981
Atlee Hammaker	P	1982-1983
Renie Martin	P	1983-1984
Bob Lacey	P	1984
Brad Gulden	C	1986
Mackey Sasser	C	1987
Kirt Manwaring	C	1987-1990
Kevin Bass	OF	1991-1992
Greg Litton	IF	1992
Dave Martinez	OF	1993
Luis Mercedes	OF	1993
Darryl Strawberry	OF	1994
J.R. Phillips	IF	1996
Carlos Alfonso	Coach	1996-1999
Ron Wotus	Coach	2006-2009
Aubrey Huff	IF	2010-2012
Tim Hudson	P	2014-2015
Ruben Tejada	IF	2016
Gordon Beckham	IF	2016
José Alguacil	Coach	2017-2018

18

Bill Rigney	Manager	1958-1960
Bob Farley	IF	1961
Don Larsen	P	1962-1964
John Pregenzer	P	1964
Bill Sorrell	OF	1967
Dave Marshall	OF	1967-1969
Russ Gibson	C	1970-1972
Damaso Blanco	IF	1973-1974
Bill Rigney	Manager	1976

Bill Madlock	IF	1977-1979
Greg Johnson	OF	1979
Duane Kuiper	IF	1982-1985
Bob Melvin	C	1986
Francisco Melendez	IF	1987-1988
Bill Bathe	C	1989-1990
Mike Benjamin	IF	1990-1995
Kim Batiste	IF	1996
Brian Johnson	C	1997-1998
Jay Canizaro	IF	1999
Russ Davis	IF	2000-2001
Jalal Leach	OF	2001
Joe Lefebvre	Coach	2002-2004
Moises Alou	OF	2005-2006
Matt Cain	P	2007-2017

19

Danny O'Connell	IF	1958
Sam Jones	P	1959-1961
Billy Pierce	P	1963-1964
Frank Johnson	OF	1966
Ty Cline	OF	1967-1968
Bob Burda	IF	1969-1970
Jim Willoughby	P	1971-1972
Jim Howarth	OF	1972-1974
Von Joshua	OF	1975-1976
Tim Foli	IF	1977
Al Holland	P	1979-1982
Bill Laskey	P	1983-1985
Roger Mason	P	1985
Lary Sorenson	P	1988
James Steels	OF	1989
Kevin Bass	OF	1990
Dave Righetti	P	1991-1993
Mark Portugal	P	1994-1995
Jay Canizaro	IF	1996
Jim Poole	P	1996-1998
Doug Mirabelli	C	1999
Dave Righetti	Coach	2000-2006
Kevin Frandsen	IF	2006-2009
Dave Righetti	Coach	2010-2011
Marco Scutaro	IF	2012-2014
Dave Righetti	Coach	2013-2017
Josh Rutledge	IF	2018

20

Retired in 2010 in honor of
Monte Irvin, OF, N.Y. Giants, 1949-1955

Daryl Spencer	IF	1958-1959
Dale Long	IF	1960
Don Choate	P	1960
Bob Nieman	OF	1962
Billy Hoeft	P	1963
Ken Henderson	OF	1965
Dick Groat	IF	1967
Bobby Bonds	OF	1968

Name	Pos	Year
Frank Johnson	OF	1968
Bernie Williams	OF	1970-1972
Glenn Redmon	IF	1974
Bobby Murcer	OF	1975
Vic Harris	IF	1977-1978
Joe Strain	IF	1979-1980
Frank Robinson	Manager	1981-1984
Jeffrey Leonard	OF	1985-1987
Phil Garner	IF	1988
Wendell Kim	Coach	1989-1996
Gene Clines	Coach	1997-2002
Tony Torcato	OF	2003
Michael Tucker	OF	2004-2005
Todd Greene	C	2006
Willie Upshaw	Coach	2007
Steve Holm	C	2008
John Bowker	OF	2009-2010

21

Name	Pos	Year
Don Taussig	OF	1958
Marshall Renfroe	P	1960
Ernie Bowman	IF	1961-1963
Gil Garrido	IF	1964
Jose Cardenal	OF	1964
Len Gabrielson	OF	1965
Warren Spahn	P	1965
Bob Garibaldi	P	1966
Don Mason	IF	1968-1970
Ed Goodson	IF	1972-1975
Ken Reitz	IF	1976
Rob Andrews	IF	1977-1979
Guy Sularz	IF	1980-1983
Tom McCraw	Coach	1984-1985
Candy Maldonado	OF	1986-1989
Mike Laga	IF	1989-1990
Royce Clayton	IF	1991
Darnell Coles	OF	1991
Kevin Rogers	P	1992
Paul Faries	IF	1993
Scott Sanderson	P	1993
Brad Brink	P	1994
Deion Sanders	OF	1995
Shawon Dunston	IF	1996
Jeff Kent	IF	1997-2002
Carlos Valderrama	IF	2003
Eric Young	IF	2003
Ruben Rivera	OF	2003
Tony Torcato	OF	2004-2005
Alex Sanchez	OF	2005
Jason Ellison	OF	2005-2006
Ryan Klesko	IF	2007
John Bowker	OF	2008-2009
Freddy Sanchez	IF	2009-2011
Nick Noonan	IF	2013
Tony Abreu	IF	2014
Tyler Colvin	OF	2014

Name	Pos	Year
Nick Noonan	IF	2015
Conor Gillaspie	IF	2016-2017
Shawon Dunston	Coach	2018

22

Name	Pos	Year
Jim King	OF	1958
Jackie Brandt	OF	1958-1959
Dan O'Connell	IF	1959
Jack Fisher	P	1963
Hal Lanier	IF	1964-1971
Damaso Blanco	IF	1972
Jim Rosario	OF	1972
Willie Montanez	IF	1975-1976
Jack Clark	OF	1976-1984
David Green	IF	1985
Will Clark	IF	1986-1993
Osvaldo Fernandez	P	1996-1997
Damon Minor	IF	2000
Eric Davis	OF	2001
Jason Schmidt	P	2002
Manny Aybar	P	2002
Kurt Ainsworth	P	2002
Jose Cruz Jr.	OF	2003
Dustan Mohr	OF	2004
Mike Matheny	C	2005-2006
Matt Morris	P	2007
Keiichi Yabu	P	2008
Eli Whiteside	C	2009-2012
Cole Gillespie	OF	2013
Roger Kieschnick	OF	2013
Dan Uggla	IF	2014
Jake Peavy	P	2014-2016
Christian Arroyo	IF	2017
Andrew McCutchen	OF	2018

23

Name	Pos	Year
Bill White	IF	1958
Felipe Alou	OF	1959-1963
Jack Hiatt	C	1965
Ken Henderson	OF	1965-1966
Tito Fuentes	IF	1967
Clyde King	Manager	1969-1970
Tito Fuentes	IF	1970-1974
Herm Starrette	Coach	1977-1978
Phil Nastu	P	1979-1980
Enos Cabell	IF	1981
Jose Barrios	P	1982
Herm Starrette	Coach	1983-1984
Jose Uribe	IF	1985-1992
Steve Scarsone	IF	1993-1996
Dante Powell	OF	1997
Ellis Burks	OF	1998-2000
Shawon Dunston	IF	2001-2002
Felipe Alou	Manager	2003-2006
Randy Messenger	P	2007
Ivan Ochoa	IF	2008
Ryan Garko	IF	2009

Name	Pos	Year
Ron Wotus	Coach	2010-2014
Jeff Francoeur	OF	2013
Nori Aoki	OF	2015
Ron Wotus	Coach	2016-2018

24

Retired in 1983 in honor of Willie Mays

Name	Pos	Year
Willie Mays	OF	1951-1957 (NY); 1958-1972 (SF)

25

Retired in 2018 in honor of Barry Bonds

Name	Pos	Year
Whitey Lockman	IF	1958
Jim Marshall	IF	1960-1961
Don Blasingame	IF	1961
Dick Estelle	P	1964-1965
Ollie Brown	OF	1966-1968
Bobby Bonds	OF	1969-1974
Rob Dressler	P	1975-1976
Bobby Murcer	OF	1976
Phil Nastu	P	1978
Dave Roberts	P	1979
Jerry Martin	OF	1981
Ron Pruitt	C	1982-1983
Dan Gladden	OF	1982-1983
Pat Larkin	P	1983
Brian Kingman	P	1983
Gene Richards	OF	1984
Mark Calvert	P	1984
Dan Driessen	IF	1985-1986
Mike Aldrete	OF	1987-1988
Tracy Jones	OF	1989
Pat Sheridan	OF	1989
Rick Leach	OF	1990
Mike Felder	OF	1991-1992
Barry Bonds	OF	1993-2007

26

Name	Pos	Year
Dusty Rhodes	OF	1958-1959
Bob Speake	OF	1958-1959
Chuck Hiller	IF	1961-1965
Tito Fuentes	IF	1965-1966
Ron Bryant	P	1969-1970
Floyd Wicker	P	1971
Dave Kingman	IF/OF	1971-1974
John Montefusco	P	1975-1980
Doyle Alexander	P	1981
Jeffrey Leonard	OF	1982-1984
Chuck Hensley	P	1986
Randy Bockus	P	1986-1987
Jessie Reid	OF	1987-1988
Charlie Hayes	IF	1989
Mike Benjamin	IF	1989
Mike Kingery	OF	1990-1991
Bill Swift	P	1992-1994
Rich Aurilia	IF	1995

Stephen Mintz	P	1995
Mark Gardner	P	1996-2001
Jay Witasick	P	2002
Mark Gardner	Coach	2003-2017
Cory Gearrin	P	2018

27

Retired in 1983 in honor of Juan Marichal

Hank Sauer	OF	1958
Bob Schmidt	C	1959
Jim Hegan	C	1959
Juan Marichal	P	1960-1973

28

Ruben Gomez	P	1958
Billy Loes	P	1960-1961
Gaylord Perry	P	1962
Bob Garibaldi	P	1962-1963
Duke Snider	OF	1964
Joe Gibbon	P	1966-1969
Bob Garibaldi	P	1969
Ron Kline	P	1969
Jerry Johnson	P	1971-1972
Ed Halicki	P	1974-1980
Mike Rowland	P	1980-1981
Andy McGaffigan	P	1982-1983
George Riley	P	1984
Jose Morales	Coach	1985-1988
Bob Knepper	P	1989-1990
Andy McGaffigan	P	1990
Ed Vosberg	P	1990
Tom Herr	IF	1991
Cory Snyder	OF	1992
Kevin Rogers	P	1993-1995
Stan Javier	OF	1996-1999
Juan Melo	IF	2000
John Vander Wal	OF	2001
David Bell	IF	2002
Lance Niekro	IF	2003
Damian Moss	P	2003
Wayne Franklin	P	2004
Lance Niekro	IF	2005-2007
Randy Messenger	P	2007
Rajai Davis	OF	2007-2008
Travis Denker	IF	2008
Buster Posey	C	2009-2018

29

Willie Kirkland	OF	1958-1960
Bob Shaw	P	1964-1966
Jack Hiatt	C	1967
Norm Siebern	IF	1967
Nate Oliver	IF	1968
Tito Fuentes	IF	1969-1970
Steve Stone	P	1972
Mike Phillips	IF	1973
Bruce Miller	IF	1974-1976

Joe Coleman	P	1979
Rich Murray	IF	1980
Alan Fowlkes	P	1982
Randy Lerch	P	1983-1984
Alex Trevino	C	1985
Candy Maldonado	OF	1986
Mike LaCoss	P	1986-1991
Rick Parker	OF	1991
Steve Hosey	OF	1992
Dan Carlson	P	1996-1997
Joe Carter	OF	1998
Scott Servais	C	1999
Bobby Estalella	C	2000-2001
Jason Schmidt	P	2001-2006
Luis Figueroa	IF	2007
Travis Blackley	P	2007
Brian Bocock	IF	2008
Scott McClain	IF	2008
Jesus Guzman	IF	2009
Ryan Rohlinger	IF	2009-2011
Bill Hall	IF	2011
Hector Sanchez	C	2011-2015
Jeff Samardzija	P	2016-2018

30

Retired in 1999 in honor of Orlando Cepeda

Orlando Cepeda	IF	1958-1966
Billy Hoeft	P	1966
Mike McCormick	P	1967
Don Carrithers	P	1970-1973
John Boccabella	C	1974
Derrel Thomas	IF	1975-1977
John Tamargo	C	1978-1979
Bob Kearney	P	1979
Chili Davis	OF	1981-1987
Rusty Tillman	OF	1988
Donell Nixon	OF	1988-1989
Mark Thurmond	P	1990
Chris James	OF	1992
Jim McNamara	C	1992-1993
Jim Deshaies	P	1993
Jamie Brewington	P	1995
Dan Peltier	IF	1996
Marcus Jensen	C	1996-1997
Jacob Cruz	OF	1997-1998
Dante Powell	OF	1998

31

Paul Giel	P	1958
Billy O'Dell	P	1960-1964
Bob Burda	IF	1965-1966
Cesar Gutierrez	IF	1967, 1969
Bob Taylor	OF	1970
Chris Arnold	IF	1971-1972
Garry Maddox	OF	1972-1975
Larry Herndon	OF	1976-1981
John Rabb	C	1982

Mike Chris	P	1982-1983
Jeff Cornell	P	1984
Bob Moore	P	1985
Rick Lancelotti	IF/OF	1986
Jessie Reid	OF	1987
Randy Bockus	P	1987-1988
Dennis Cook	P	1988-1989
Don Robinson	P	1990-1991
Jim Pena	P	1992
J.R. Phillips	IF	1993
Erik Johnson	IF	1993-1994
Mark Leiter	P	1995-1996
Desi Wilson	IF	1996
Robb Nen	P	1998-2002
Vinnie Chulk	P	2006-2008
Brad Penny	P	2009
Hensley Meulens	Coach	2010-2011
Brad Penny	P	2012
Hensley Meulens	Coach	2013-2018

32

Al Worthington	P	1958-1960
Dave Philley	OF	1960
Carl Boles	OF	1962-1963
Bill Hands	P	1965
Ron Bryant	P	1967
Don Carrithers	P	1970
Ron Bryant	P	1971-1974
Jake Brown	OF	1975
Tom Heintzelman	IF	1977-1978
Ed Whitson	P	1979-1981
Rich Gale	P	1982
Wallace Johnson	IF	1983
Mike Vail	OF	1983
Mark Calvert	P	1983
Dan Gladden	OF	1984-1986
Steve Carlton	P	1986
Craig Lefferts	P	1987-1989
Brad Komminsk	OF	1990
John Burkett	P	1990
Rick Parker	OF	1991
Trevor Wilson	P	1992-1995
Bill Mueller	IF	1996-2000
Kurt Ainsworth	P	2001-2002
Bill Mueller	IF	2002
Kurt Ainsworth	P	2003
Dustin Hermanson	P	2003-2004
Brian Dallimore	IF	2005
LaTroy Hawkins	P	2005
Kevin Correia	P	2006-2008
Dave Righetti	Coach	2009
Ryan Vogelsong	P	2011-2015
Vin Mazzaro	P	2016
Steven Okert	P	2017

33

Name	Position	Years
Jack Sanford	P	1959-1965
Frank Johnson	OF	1967-1968
Ron Hunt	IF	1968-1970
Steve Stone	P	1971
Jim Barr	P	1971-1978
Bill Bordley	P	1980
Allen Ripley	P	1980-1981
Doyle Alexander	P	1981
Jim Barr	P	1982-1983
Alex Sanchez	OF	1984
Roger Craig	Manager	1986-1987
Ron Davis	P	1988
Stuart Tate	P	1988
Russ Swan	P	1989
John Burkett	P	1990-1994
Steve Bourgeois	P	1996
Rich Rodriguez	P	1996-1999
Benito Santiago	C	2001-2003
Ricky Ledee	OF	2004
David Aardsma	P	2004
Justin Knoedler	C	2005
Al Levine	P	2005
Brian Wilson	P	2006-2007
Aaron Rowand	OF	2008-2011
Charlie Culberson	IF	2012
Dave Righetti	Coach	2012-2015
Decker Steve	Coach	2015-2017
Alonzo Powell	Coach	2018

34

Name	Position	Years
John Orsino	C	1961-1962
Ron Herbel	P	1963-1969
Ed Goodson	IF	1970-1971
John D'Acquisto	P	1973-1976
Tom Heintzelman	IF	1977-1978
Terry Cornutt	P	1977-1978
Pedro Borbon	P	1979
Mike Krukow	P	1983
Mark Grant	P	1984
Norm Sherry	Coach	1986-1991
Dave Burba	P	1992-1995
Scott Service	P	1995
Allen Watson	P	1996
Glenallen Hill	OF	1997
Ramon Martinez	IF	1998-2002
Jesse Foppert	P	2003-2005
Daniel Ortmeier	OF	2005
Steve Kline	P	2006-2007
Billy Sadler	P	2008
Matt Downs	IF	2010
Darren Ford	OF	2010-2011
Clay Hensley	P	2012
Guillermo Moscoso	P	2013
David Huff	P	2014
Andrew Susac	C	2014-2015
Chris Stratton	P	2017-2018

35

Name	Position	Years
Pete Burnside	P	1958
John Fitzgerald	P	1958
Georges Maranda	P	1960
Billy Pierce	P	1962
Frank Linzy	P	1963, 1965-1970
Jerry Johnson	P	1970
Chris Speier	IF	1971-1977
Art Gardner	OF	1978
Dennis Littlejohn	C	1979-1980
Tom O'Malley	IF	1982-1984
Chris Brown	IF	1984-1987
Chris Speier	IF	1987-1989
Andres Santana	IF	1990
Steve Decker	C	1991-1992
Larry Carter	P	1993
Salomon Torres	P	1993-1995
Carlos Valdez	P	1995
Rich Aurilia	IF	1996-2003
Deivi Cruz	IF	2004-2005
Brett Tomko	P	2005
Matt Morris	P	2006
Rich Aurilia	IF	2007
Brandon Crawford	IF	2011-2018

36

Retired in 2005 in honor of Gaylord Perry

Name	Position	Years
Joe Shipley	P	1958
Billy Muffett	P	1959
Bud Byerly	P	1959-1960
Sherman Jones	P	1960
Gaylord Perry	P	1963-1971
Jim Howarth	OF	1971
Sam McDowell	P	1972
Gary Matthews	OF	1972-1976
Skip James	IF	1977-1978
Jim Dwyer	OF	1978
Bill North	OF	1979-1981
Dan Schatzeder	P	1982
Brad Wellman	IF	1982-1986
Tom McCraw	Coach	1983
Keith Comstock	P	1987
Dennis Cook	P	1988
Rafael Novoa	P	1990
Gil Heredia	P	1991-1992
Steve Reed	P	1992
Gino Minutelli	P	1993
Rick Layana	P	1993
Tony Menendez	P	1994
Kenny Greer	P	1995
Shawn Estes	P	1995
Jay Canizaro	IF	1996
Armando Rios	IF	1998
Joe Nathan	P	1999-2000, 2002-2003
A.J. Pierzynski	C	2004

37

Name	Position	Years
Stu Miller	P	1958-1962
Masanori Murakami	P	1965
Ray Sadecki	P	1966-1969
Steve Whitaker	OF	1970
Frank Johnson	OF	1970
Mike Caldwell	P	1974-1976
Ed Plank	P	1978-1979
Jeff Ransom	C	1983
Randy Gomez	C	1984
Kelly Downs	P	1986-1992
Andy Allanson	C	1993
Terry Bross	P	1993
Chris Hook	P	1995-1996
Joe Roa	P	1997
John Johnstone	P	1997
Miguel Del Toro	P	1999
Damon Minor	OF	2001-2002
Alberto Castillo	C	2003
Brian Cooper	P	2004
Merkin Valdez	P	2004
Jack Taschner	P	2005-2008
Matt Downs	IF	2009
Dan Runzler	P	2009
Todd Wellemeyer	P	2010
Chris Stewart	C	2011
Hensley Meulens	Coach	2012
Dan Otero	P	2012-2013
Kensuke Tanaka	IF	2013
Adam Duvall	IF	2014
Kelby Tomlinson	IF	2015-2018

38

Name	Position	Years
Joe Shipley	P	1958
Gordon Jones	P	1958-1959
Billy Loes	P	1960
Manuel Mota	OF	1962
Bob Hendley	P	1964-1965
Bob Priddy	P	1965-1966
Wes Westrum	Coach	1968
Bill Faul	P	1970
Lee Pitlock	P	1970
Steve Hamilton	P	1971
Elias Sosa	P	1972-1974
Horace Speed	OF	1975
Greg Minton	P	1977-1987
Roger Craig	Manager	1988-1992
Rikkert Faneyte	OF	1993-1994
Pat Gomez	P	1994-1995
Jose Bautista	P	1995-1996
Jeff Ball	IF	1998
Aaron Fultz	P	2000-2002
Jim Brower	P	2003-2005
Brandon Puffer	P	2005
Matt Kinney	P	2005
Justin Knoedler	C	2006
Mike Stanton	P	2006

Brian Wilson	P	2008-2012
Heath Hembree	P	2013
Michael Morse	OF	2014
Brett Bochy	P	2015
Grant Green	IF	2016
Michael Morse	OF	2017
Tyler Beede	P	2018

39

Leon Wagner	OF	1958
Curt Barclay	P	1958-1959
Eddie Fisher	P	1959, 1961
Dick LeMay	P	1961-1962
Randy Hundley	C	1964-1965
Lindy McDaniel	P	1966-1968
Bill Monbouquette	P	1968
Frank Reberger	P	1970-1972
Randy Moffitt	P	1972-1975
Bob Knepper	P	1976-1980
Tom O'Malley	IF	1982
Renie Martin	P	1982
Mike Krukow	P	1983-1989
Tony Perezchica	IF	1990-1991
Ted Wood	OF	1991-1993
Paul Faries	IF	1994
Rikkert Faneyte	OF	1994
Allen Watson	P	1996
Roberto Hernandez	P	1997
Steve Reed	P	1998
Pedro Feliz	IF	2000-2003
Todd Linden	OF	2004-2007
LaTroy Hawkins	P	2005
Guillermo Rodriguez	C	2007
Roberto Kelly	Coach	2008-2016
Justin Ruggiano	OF	2017
Carlos Moncrief	OF	2017
Rick Schu	Coach	2018

40

Mike McCormick	P	1958-1962
John Pregenzer	P	1963
Ozzie Virgil	IF/Coach	1966
Mike McCormick	P	1967-1970
John Cumberland	P	1970-1972
Tom Bradley	P	1973-1975
John Curtis	P	1977-1979
Al Hargesheimer	P	1980-1981
Jose Barrios	OF	1982
Mark Dempsey	P	1982
Dave LaPoint	P	1985
Juan Berenguer	P	1986
John Burkett	P	1987
Don Robinson	P	1987-1989
Steve Bedrosian	P	1989-1990
Bud Black	P	1991-1994
Mark Dewey	P	1995-1996
Wilson Alvarez	P	1997

Jason Christiansen	P	2001-2005
Doug Clark	OF	2005
Daniel Ortmeier	OF	2006-2008
Madison Bumgarner	P	2009-2018

41

Ramon Monzant	P	1958, 1960
Matty Alou	OF	1960-1965
Don Mason	IF	1966-1968
Mike Davison	P	1969-1970
Miguel Puente	P	1970
Jim Howarth	OF	1971
Don Rose	P	1974
Greg Minton	P	1975
Darrell Evans	IF	1976-1983
Scot Thompson	IF	1984-1985
Mike Woodard	IF	1985-1987
Dave Henderson	OF	1987
John Burkett	P	1987
Trevor Wilson	P	1988-1991
Bryan Hickerson	P	1991-1994
Sergio Valdez	P	1995
Rich DeLucia	P	1996-1997
Cory Bailey	P	1997-1998
Scott Linebrink	P	2000
Chad Zerbe	P	2000-2003
Brad Hennessey	P	2004-2008
Jeremy Affeldt	P	2009-2015
Mark Melancon	P	2017-2018

42

Retired in 1997 in honor of Jackie Robinson

Marv Grissom	P	1958
Joe Shipley	P	1960
Bob Bolin	P	1961-1969
John Morris	P	1972
Jim Willoughby	P	1973-1974
Greg Minton	P	1976-1977
Terry Cornutt	P	1978
Milt May	C	1980
John Van Ornum	Coach	1981-1984
Jack Mull	Coach	1985
Bill Fahey	Coach	1986-1991
Mike Jackson	P	1992-1994
John Roper	P	1995
Keith Williams	OF	1996
Kirk Rueter	P	1996-1997

43

Johnny Antonelli	P	1958-1960
Bob Barton	C	1965
Don Landrum	OF	1966
Ken Henderson	OF	1967
Rich Robertson	P	1967-1968
Jim Rosario	OF	1971-1972
Charlie Williams	P	1972
John Morris	P	1973-1974

Steve Barber	P	1974
Glenn Adams	OF	1975-1976
Tom Griffin	P	1979-1981
Scott Garrelts	P	1982-1983
Gary Rajsich	OF	1985
Dave Dravecky	P	1987-1989
Carl Bottenfield	P	1994
Jeff Juden	P	1996
Rene Arocha	P	1997
Danny Darwin	P	1997-1998
Jerry Spradlin	P	1999
Ryan Jensen	P	2001
Brian Boehringer	P	2001
Ryan Jensen	P	2002-2003
Sidney Ponson	P	2003
Dave Burba	P	2004
Matt Cain	P	2005-2006
Geno Espineli	P	2008
Alex Hinshaw	P	2009-2010
Orlando Cabrera	IF	2011
Dan Otero	P	2012
Sandy Rosario	P	2013
Jake Peavy	P	2014
Brett Bochy	P	2014
Kevin Frandsen	IF	2015
Justin Maxwell	OF	2015
Tim Federowicz	C	2017
Curt Young	Coach	2018

44

Retired in 1980 in honor of Willie McCovey

Don Johnson	P	1958
Ray Crone	P	1958
Willie McCovey	IF/OF	1959-1973, 1977-1980

45

Nick Testa	Coach	1958
Dom Zanni	P	1958-1959
Jim Duffalo	P	1961-1965
Bill Henry	P	1965-1968
Rich Robertson	P	1969-1971
Dave Kingman	OF	1971
Frank Riccelli	P	1976
Terry Whitfield	OF	1977-1980
Bill Laskey	P	1982
Rob Deer	OF	1984-1985
Terry Mulholland	P	1986, 1988-1989
Jim Weaver	OF	1989
Francisco Olivares	P	1990-1992
Mark Carreon	OF/IF	1993-1996
Kirk Rueter	P	1997
Terry Mulholland	P	1997
Dean Hartgraves	P	1998
Chris Brock	P	1999
Todd Worrell	P	2001-2003

Tyler Walker	P	2004-2005
Todd Worrell	P	2006
Tyler Walker	P	2007-2008
Justin Miller	P	2009
Dan Runzler	P	2010-2012
Travis Ishikawa	IF/OF	2014-2015
Alejandro DeAza	OF	2015
Matt Moore	P	2016-2017
Derek Holland	P	2018

46

Joe Shipley	P	1959
Larry Jansen	Coach	1961-1971
Andy Gilbert	Coach	1972
Gary Lavelle	P	1974-1984
Jim Gott	P	1985
Jon Perlman	P	1987
Craig Colbert	C	1992-1993
Steve Frey	P	1994-1995
Terry Mulholland	P	1995
Rich DeLucia	P	1996
Kirk Rueter	P	1997-2005
Dave Righetti	Coach	2006-2008
Bob Howry	P	2009
Santiago Casilla	P	2010-2016
Orlando Calixte	IF	2017
Drew Stubbs	OF	2017

47

Nick Testa	C	1958
Bob Etheridge	IF	1967
Nestor Chavez	P	1967
Don McMahon	P	1969-1972
Don McMahon	Coach/P	1973-1975
Lynn McGlothen	P	1977-1978
Dennis Littlejohn	C	1978
Don McMahon	Coach	1980-1982
Frank Williams	P	1984-1986
Joe Price	P	1987-1989
Steve Decker	C	1990
Dan Quisenberry	P	1990
Rod Beck	P	1991-1997
Jose Mesa	P	1998
Felix Rodriguez	P	1999-2004
David Aardsma	P	2004
Scott Eyre	P	2005
Tyler Walker	P	2006
Scott Munter	P	2007
Merkin Valdez	P	2008-2009
Chris Ray	P	2010
Eric Surkamp	P	2011-2013
Jarrett Parker	OF	2015
Johnny Cueto	P	2016-2018

48

Jim Constable	P	1958
Leon Wagner	OF	1958-1959

Jim Constable	P	1963
Al Stanek	P	1963
Ollie Brown	OF	1965
Rich Robertson	P	1966
Sam McDowell	P	1972-1973
Butch Metzger	P	1974
Fred Breining	P	1980-1983
Bob Miller	Coach	1985
Roger Mason	P	1986
Rick Reuschel	P	1987-1991
Paul McClellan	P	1991
Pat Rapp	P	1992
Dick Pole	Coach	1993-1997
Russ Ortiz	P	1998-2002
Matt Herges	P	2003-2005
Jack Taschner	P	2005
Jamey Wright	P	2006
Russ Ortiz	P	2007
Erick Threets	P	2008
Pablo Sandoval	IF/C	2008-2014
Steven Okert	P	2016-2017
Pablo Sandoval	IF/C	2017-2018

49

Felipe Alou	OF	1958
Ron Bryant	P	1967
Jim Johnson	P	1970
Rich Robertson	P	1971
Sam Dyson	P	2017-2018

50

Bob Schroder	IF	1965
John Montefusco	P	1974
Jeff Stember	P	1980
Scott Garrelts	P	1983-1991*
Greg Brummett	P	1993
William VanLandingham	P	1994-1997
Julian Tavarez	P	1998-1999
Manny Aybar	P	2002-2003
Alberto Castillo	C	2003
Todd Linden	OF	2003
Kevin Correia	P	2003
Brett Tomko	P	2004-2005
Eliezer Alfonzo	C	2006-2008
Conor Gillaspie	IF	2008
Matt Palmer	P	2008
Conor Gillaspie	IF	2011-2012
Jose Mijares	P	2012-2013
Matt Duffy	IF	2014-2015
Ryan Lollis	OF	2015
Ty Blach	P	2016-2018

51

Tommy Toms	P	1975-1977
Matt Nokes	C	1985
Jim Gott	P	1985-1987
Rick Parker	OF	1990

Greg Booker	P	1990
Willie McGee	OF	1991-1994
Enrique Burgos	P	1995
Doug Creek	P	1996-1997
Chris Brock	P	1998
Jerry Spradlin	P	1999
Ryan Vogelsong	P	2000
Troy Brohawn	P	2002
Brian Powell	P	2003
Noah Lowry	P	2004-2008
Randy Johnson	P	2009
Justin Christian	OF	2011-2012
Eric Hacker	P	2012
Jake Dunning	P	2013-2014
Erik Cordier	P	2014
Mac Williamson	OF	2015-2017

52

Chris Bourjos	OF	1980
Mark Grant	P	1986-1987
Russ Swan	P	1989-1990
Larry Carter	P	1993
Jeff Reed	C	1993-1995
Julian Tavarez	P	1997
Alvin Morman	P	1998
Felipe Crespo	IF	2000-2001
Trey Lunsford	C	2002-2003
Justin Knoedler	C	2004
Brian Cooper	P	2005
Scott Atchison	P	2007
Alex Hinshaw	P	2008
Brandon Medders	P	2009-2010
Ramon Ramirez	P	2010-2011
Yusmeiro Petit	P	2012-2015
Ramon Ramirez	P	2013
Miguel Gomez	IF	2017

53

Mike Rowland	P	1980
Alan Fowlkes	P	1982
Colin Ward	P	1985
Eric Gunderson	P	1990-1991
Joe Rosselli	P	1995
Keith Foulke	P	1997
Orel Hershiser	P	1998
Kevin Correia	P	2003-2005
Leo Estrella	P	2004
Jonathan Sanchez	P	2006-2008
Denny Bautista	P	2010
Melky Cabrera	OF	2012
Ehire Adrianza	IF	2013-2014
Chris Heston	P	2014-2016
Austin Slater	OF	2017

54

Angel Escobar	P	1988
Rich Gossage	P	1989

Tim Scott	P	1996
Kevin Walker	P	2004
Scott Munter	P	2005-2007
Sergio Romo	P	2008-2016
Reyes Moronta	P	2017-2018

55

Gordie MacKenzie	Coach	1986-1988
Randy O'Neal	P	1990
Rich Monteleone	P	1994
Shawn Estes	P	1996-2001
Luis Pujols	Coach	2003-2006
Tim Lincecum	P	2007-2015

56

Pete Falcone	P	1975
Frank Funk	Coach	1976
Joe Pittman	IF	1984
Andres Santana	IF	1991-1993
Dax Jones	OF	1996
Alan Embree	P	1999-2001
Dante Powell	OF	2001
Jason Ellison	OF	2003-2005
Dan Giese	P	2007
Osiris Matos	P	2008
Ryan Sadowski	P	2009
Andres Torres	OF	2010-2011
Travis Blackley	P	2012
Andres Torres	OF	2013
Gary Brown	OF	2014
Trevor Brown	C	2015
Albert Suarez	P	2016-2017
Tony Watson	P	2018

57

Doug Henry	P	1997, 2000
Ben Weber	P	2000
Jerome Williams	P	2003-2005
Julio Ramirez	OF	2005
Eugenio Velez	OF	2007
Ryan Rohlinger	IF	2008
Jonathan Sanchez	P	2009-2011
Francisco Peguero	OF	2012
Chad Gaudin	P	2013
Juan Gutierrez	P	2014
Mike Broadway	P	2015-2016
Matt Reynolds	P	2016
Bryan Morris	P	2017
Dan Slania	P	2017

58

Roger Samuels	P	1988
Denny Sommers	Coach	1993-1994
Bill Hayes	Coach	2007-2017
Pierce Johnson	P	2018

59

Rick Rodriguez	P	1990
Juan Lopez	Coach	1996-2002
Justin Knoedler	C	2005
Jeremy Accardo	P	2005-2006
Billy Sadler	P	2006
Andres Torres	OF	2009
Guillermo Mota	P	2010-2012
Mike Kickham	P	2013
Cody Hall	P	2015
Neil Ramirez	P	2017
Kyle Crick	P	2017
Andrew Suarez	P	2018

60

Dave Heaverlo	P	1975-1977
Russ Ortiz	P	1998
Francisco Santos	IF/OF	2003
Noah Lowry	P	2003
Brian Dallimore	IF	2004
Justin Knoedler	C	2006
Erick Threets	P	2007
Waldis Joaquin	P	2009-2011
Hunter Strickland	P	2014-2018

61

Livan Hernandez	P	1999-2002
Shane Loux	P	2012
Josh Osich	P	2015-2018

62

Wilson Delgado	IF	1996-1997, 1999-2000
Cory Gearrin	P	2015-2017

63

Jean Machi	P	2012-2015
Ryder Jones	IF	2017

64

Manny Aybar	P	2002
Derek Law	P	2016-2017

65

Steve Soderstrom	P	1996
Steve Edlefsen	P	2011-2012

66

Doug Mirabelli	C	1996-1997
Gorkys Hernandez	OF	2016-2017

67

Todd Linden	OF	2003
Roberto Gomez	P	2017-2018

68

Xavier Nady	OF	2012
Chris Stratton	P	2016

70

Willie Upshaw	Coach	2005-2006
Justin Christian	OF	2011
Joe Lefebvre	Coach	2012
George Kontos	P	2012-2017
Julian Fernandez	P	2018

71

Pat Misch	P	2006-2007

72

Luis Aquino	P	1995

74

Joe Nathan	P	2016

75

Barry Zito	P	2007-2013

77

Matt Herges	Coach	2018

79

Jean Machi	P	2012

87

Dan Otero	P	2012

88

Eli Whiteside	Coach	2018

3
Bill Terry

4
Mel Ott

11
Carl Hubbell

20
Monte Irvin

3 4
11 20

ALL-TIME UNIFORM NUMBERS
ALPHABETICAL ORDER

NAME	NUMBERS
A	
David Aardsma	33, 47
Tony Abreu	10, 21
Jeremy Accardo	59
Glenn Adams	43
Ehire Adrianza	53, 6, 1, 13
Jeremy Affeldt	41
Kurt Ainsworth	32, 22
Mike Aldrete	1, 25
Doyle Alexander	26, 33
Gary Alexander	14
Carlos Alfonso	16, 17
Edgardo Alfonzo	13, 12
Eliezer Alfonzo	50
José Alguacil	17
Andy Allanson	37
Felipe Alou	49, 23
Jesus Alou	14
Matty Alou	41
Moises Alou	18
Joe Altobelli	6
Wilson Alvarez	40
Joe Amalfitano	14, 5
Dave Anderson	10
Rob Andrews	21
Johnny Antonelli	43
Nori Aoki	23
Luis Aquino	72
Joaquin Arias	13
Chris Arnold	31, 17, 15
Rene Arocha	43
Christian Arroyo	22
Scott Atchison	52
Rich Aurilia	26, 35
Manny Aybar	22, 50, 64
B	
Cory Bailey	41
Ed Bailey	6
Dusty Baker	12
Jeff Ball	38
Steve Barber	43
Curt Barclay	39
Jim Barr	33
Jose Barrios	23, 40
Bob Barton	43, 1
Shawn Barton	14
Kevin Bass	19, 17
Bill Bathe	18

Kim Batiste	18
Denny Bautista	53
Jose Bautista	38
Rod Beck	47
Gordon Beckham	17
Steve Bedrosian	40
Tyler Beede	38
David Bell	28
Brandon Belt	9
Carlos Beltran	15
Marvin Benard	7
Mike Benjamin	26, 18
Vern Benson	8
Todd Benzinger	14
Juan Berenguer	40
Dave Bergman	16
Damon Berryhill	8
Dick Bertell	6
Ty Blach	50
Bud Black	40
Travis Blackley	29, 56
Damaso Blanco	22, 18
Gregor Blanco	7, 1
Don Blasingame	10, 25
Vida Blue	14
John Boccabella	30
Brett Bochy	43, 38
Bruce Bochy	15, 16
Randy Bockus	26, 31
Brian Bocock	29
Brian Boehringer	43
Carl Boles	32
Bob Bolin	42
Barry Bonds	25
Bobby Bonds	20, 25,16
Greg Booker	51
Pedro Borbon	34
Bill Bordley	33
Carl Bottenfield	43
Steve Bourgeois	33
Chris Bourjos	52
John Bowker	21, 20
Ernie Bowman	21
Tom Bradley	40
Jackie Brandt	22
Fred Breining	48
Bob Brenly	15
Ed Bressoud	16

Jamie Brewington	30
Rocky Bridges	6
Brad Brink	21
Dave Bristol	1, 5
Mike Broadway	57
Chris Brock	51, 45
Troy Brohawn	51
Terry Bross	37
Jim Brower	38
Chris Brown	35
Gary Brown	56
Jake Brown	32
Ollie Brown	48, 25
Trevor Brown	56, 14
Greg Brummett	50
Ron Bryant	32, 49, 26
Don Buford	9, 6
Madison Bumgarner	40
Dave Burba	34, 43
Bob Burda	31, 19
Enrique Burgos	51
John Burkett	40, 41, 32, 33
Ellis Burks	23
Pete Burnside	35
Pat Burrell	9, 5
Emmanuel Burriss	7, 16, 2
Brett Butler	2
Bud Byerly	36
Marlon Byrd	6
C	
Enos Cabell	23
Melky Cabrera	53
Orlando Cabrera	6, 43
Matt Cain	43, 18
Mike Caldwell	37
Orlando Calixte	46
Mark Calvert	32, 25
Ernie Camacho	13
Jay Canizaro	19, 36, 18
Jose Cardenal	10, 21
Dan Carlson	29
Steve Carlton	32
Mark Carreon	45
Don Carrithers	30, 32
Gary Carter	8
Joe Carter	29
Larry Carter	35, 52
Santiago Casilla	46

Alberto Castillo	37, 50
Jose Castillo	12
Orlando Cepeda	30
Angel Chavez	1
Nestor Chavez	47
Don Choate	20
Mike Chris	31
Justin Christian	51, 70
Jason Christiansen	40
Vinnie Chulk	31
Doug Clark	40
Jack Clark	15, 38, 22
Will Clark	22
Royce Clayton	21, 10
Ty Cline	19
Gene Clines	20
Jim Coker	2
Craig Colbert	46
Joe Coleman	29
Darnell Coles	21
Tylor Colvin	10, 21
Keith Comstock	36
Jim Constable	40
Dennis Cook	31, 36
Brian Cooper	37, 52
Erik Cordier	51
Jeff Cornell	31
Terry Cornutt	34, 42
Kevin Correia	50, 53, 32
Roger Craig	33, 38
Del Crandall	9
Brandon Crawford	35
Doug Creek	51
Felipe Crespo	52
Kyle Crick	59
Ray Crone	44
Deivi Cruz	10, 35
Hector "Heity" Cruz	9
Jacob Cruz	30
Jose Cruz Jr.	22
Johnny Cueto	47
Charlie Culberson	33
John Cumberland	40
John Curtis	40

D

John D'Acquisto	34
Brian Dallimore	14, 60, 2, 32
Alvin Dark	1
Danny Darwin	43
Jim Davenport	12, 9, 1, 15
Chili Davis	30
Eric Davis	22
Mark Davis	13
Rajai Davis	28
Ron Davis	33
Russ Davis	18

Mike Davison	41
Tomas De la Rosa	10
Alejandro DeAza	45
Steve Decker	47, 35
Rob Deer	45
Ivan DeJesus	9
Miguel Del Toro	37
Wilson Delgado	62, 1
Rich DeLucia	41, 46
Mark Dempsey	40
Travis Denker	28
Mark DeRosa	7
Jim Deshaies	30
Mark Dewey	14, 40
Alex Diaz	1
Dick Dietz	2
Chris Dominguez	10
Kelly Downs	37
Matt Downs	37, 34
Dave Dravecky	43
Rob Dressler	25
Dan Driessen	25
Jim Duffalo	45
Frank Duffy	14
Matt Duffy	50, 5
Jake Dunning	51
Shawon Dunston	21, 8, 23
Ray Durham	5
Adam Duvall	37
Jim Dwyer	36
Sam Dyson	49

E

Steve Edlefsen	65
Randy Elliott	16
Jason Ellison	56, 21
Alan Embree	56
Angel Escobar	54
Geno Espineli	43
Bobby Estalella	29
Dick Estelle	25
Shawn Estes	36, 55
Leo Estrella	53
Bob Etheridge	47, 17
Darrell Evans	41
Scott Eyre	47

F

Bill Fahey	42
Pete Falcone	56
Rikkert Faneyte	38, 39
Paul Faries	31, 39
Bob Farley	18
Jeff Fassero	14
Bill Faul	38
Tim Federowicz	43
Mike Felder	25

Pedro Feliz	39, 7
Julian Fernandez	70
Osvaldo Fernandez	22
Jesus Figueroa	1
Luis Figueroa	29
Jim Finigan	17
Steve Finley	12
Eddie Fisher	39, 7
Jack Fisher	22
John Fitzgerald	35
Tim Flannery	6, 1
Tim Foli	19
Mike Fontenot	14
Jesse Foppert	34
Darren Ford	34
George Foster	14
Keith Foulke	53
Alan Fowlkes	29, 53
Charlie Fox	9, 7
Jeff Francoeur	23
Kevin Frandsen	8, 19, 43
Wayne Franklin	28
Herman Franks	3, 6
Steve Frey	46
Tito Fuentes	26, 23, 29
Aaron Fultz	38
Frank Funk	56

G

Len Gabrielson	7, 21
Rich Gale	32
Al Gallagher	10
Andres Gallaraga	14
Art Gardner	35
Mark Gardner	26
Bob Garibaldi	28, 21
Ryan Garko	23
Phil Garner	20
Scott Garrelts	43, 50
Gil Garrido	21
Chad Gaudin	57
Cory Gearrin	62, 26
Joe Gibbon	28
Russ Gibson	18
Paul Giel	31
Dan Giese	56
Andy Gilbert	46, 8
Conor Gillaspie	50, 21
Cole Gillespie	22
Dan Gladden	25, 32
Gene Glynn	15
Wayne Gomes	2
Miguel Gomez	52
Pat Gomez	38
Randy Gomez	37
Roberto Gomez	67
Ruben Gomez	28

Ed Goodson	34, 21	Ron Herbel	34	Greg Johnson	18
Tom Goodwin	8	Gil Heredia	36	Jerry Johnson	35, 28
Rich Gossage	54	Matt Herges	48, 77	Jim Johnson	49
Jim Gott	46, 51	Dustin Hermanson	32	Pierce Johnson	58
Mark Grant	34, 52	Gorkys Hernandez	66, 7	Randy Johnson	51
David Green	22	Livan Hernandez	61	Wallace Johnson	5, 32
Grant Green	38	Roberto Hernandez	39	John Johnstone	37
Todd Greene	20	Larry Herndon	31	Chris Jones	2
Kenny Greer	36	Tom Herr	28	Dax Jones	56
Tom Griffin	43	Orel Hershiser	53	Gordon Jones	38
Marquis Grissom	9	Chris Heston	53	Ryder Jones	63
Marv Grissom	42	Jack Hiatt	2, 23, 7, 29	Sam Jones	19
Dick Groat	20	Bryan Hickerson	41	Sherman Jones	36
Jose Guillen	1, 6	Brandon Hicks	14	Tracy Jones	25
Brad Gulden	10, 17	Aaron Hill	7	Von Joshua	19
Eric Gunderson	53	Glenallen Hill	1, 34	Jeff Juden	43
Cesar Gutierrez	17, 31	Marc Hill	2	Ed Jurak	8
Juan Gutierrez	57	Shea Hillenbrand	8		
Edwards Guzman	2, 9, 13	Chuck Hiller	26, 2	**K**	
Jesus Guzman	13, 29	Alex Hinshaw	52, 43	Bob Kearney	30
		Billy Hoeft	20, 30	Roberto Kelly	39
H		Al Holland	19	Terry Kennedy	15, 16
Yamid Haad	8	Derek Holland	45	Jeff Kent	21
Eric Hacker	51	Steve Holm	20	Jeff Keppinger	8
Ed Halicki	28	Chris Hook	37	Mike Kickham	59
Bill Hall	29	Steve Hosey	29	Roger Kieschnick	22
Cody Hall	59	Jim Howarth	36, 41, 19	Wendell Kim	20
Mel Hall	2	Bob Howry	46	Clyde King	23
Tom Haller	8	Trenidad Hubbard	14	Jim King	22
Darryl Hamilton	5	Tim Hudson	17	Mike Kingery	26
Steve Hamilton	38	Aubrey Huff	17	Brian Kingman	25
Atlee Hammaker	17, 14, 7	David Huff	34	Dave Kingman	26, 45
Jeffrey Hammonds	16, 12	Nick Hundley	5	Matt Kinney	38
Bill Hands	32	Randy Hundley	39, 1	Willie Kirkland	29
Al Hargesheimer	40	Ron Hunt	33	Ryan Klesko	21
John Harrell	9	Jae-gyun Hwang	1	Ron Kline	28
Vic Harris	20			Steve Kline	34
Jim Ray Hart	16	**I**		Bob Knepper	39, 28
Dean Hartgraves	45	Travis Ishikawa	1, 5, 10, 45	Justin Knoedler	52, 33, 59, 38, 60
LaTroy Hawkins	32, 39	Mike Ivie	15	Brad Komminsk	32
Bill Hayes	58			George Kontos	70
Charlie Hayes	26, 13	**J**		Mike Krukow	34, 39
Fran Healy	6	Ray Jablonski	10	Harvey Kuenn	7
Dave Heaverlo	60	Austin Jackson	16	Duane Kuiper	18
Jim Hegan	27	Mike Jackson	42	Randy Kutcher	9
Tom Heintzelman	32, 34	Sonny Jackson	15, 16		
Bob Heise	17	Chris James	14, 30	**L**	
Heath Hembree	38	Skip James	36	Bob Lacey	17
Dave Henderson	41	Larry Jansen	46	Mike LaCoss	29
Ken Henderson	20, 23, 15, 43	Stan Javier	28	Mike Laga	21
Bob Hendley	38	Marcus Jensen	30	Rick Lancellotti	9
Brad Hennessey	41	Ryan Jensen	15, 43	Rick Lancelotti	31
Bill Henry	45	Waldis Joaquin	60	Hobie Landrith	3, 5
Doug Henry	57	Brian Johnson	18	Don Landrum	43
Chuck Hensley	26	Don Johnson	44	Hal Lanier	22
Clay Hensley	34	Erik Johnson	31	Carney Lansford	9
		Frank Johnson	19, 33, 20, 37	Dave LaPoint	40

Norm Larker	16
Pat Larkin	25
Don Larsen	18
Bill Laskey	45, 19
Harry "Cookie" Lavagetto	8
Gary Lavelle	46
Derek Law	64
Rick Layana	36
Jalal Leach	18
Rick Leach	25
Mike Leake	13
Ricky Ledee	33
Jim Lefebvre	5
Joe Lefebvre	18, 16, 70, 5
Craig Lefferts	32
Mark Leiter	31
Johnnie LeMaster	10
Dick LeMay	30
Jeffrey Leonard	26, 20, 00
Mark Leonard	1, 2
Randy Lerch	29
Al Levine	33
Darren Lewis	2
Fred Lewis	14
Mark Lewis	14
Bob Lillis	5
Tim Lincecum	55
Todd Linden	50, 67, 39
Scott Linebrink	41
Frank Linzy	35
Dennis Littlejohn	47, 35
Greg Litton	15, 17
Whitey Lockman	25, 3
Billy Loes	28, 38
Kenny Lofton	1
Ryan Lollis	50
Dale Long	7, 20
Evan Longoria	10
Juan Lopez	59
Shane Loux	61
Harry "Peanuts" Lowery	6
Terrell Lowery	14
Noah Lowry	60, 51
Trey Lunsford	52

M

Jean Machi	63, 79
Gordie MacKenzie	55
Garry Maddox	31
Bill Madlock	18
Candy Maldonado	21, 29
Kirt Manwaring	17, 8
Georges Maranda	35
Juan Marichal	27
Dave Marshall	18
Jim Marshall	25

Jerry Martin	25
Renie Martin	39, 17
Dave Martinez	17, 1
Ramon Martinez	34
Don Mason	41, 21
Roger Mason	19, 48
Mike Matheny	22
Osiris Matos	56
Gary Matthews	36
Justin Maxwell	43
Milt May	7, 42
Brent Mayne	9
Willie Mays	24
Vin Mazzaro	32
Roger McCardell	8
David McCarty	10
Scott McClain	8, 29
Paul McClellan	48
Mike McCormick	40, 30
Willie McCovey	44
Tom McCraw	36, 21
Andrew McCutchen	22
Lindy McDaniel	39
Sam McDowell	36, 48
Andy McGaffigan	28
Willie McGee	51
Casey McGehee	14
Lynn McGlothen	47
Don McMahon	47
Jim McNamara	30
John McNamara	1
Brandon Medders	52
Mark Melancon	41
Francisco Melendez	18
Juan Melo	28
Bob Melvin	7, 18
Tony Menendez	36
Luis Mercedes	17
Jose Mesa	47
Randy Messenger	23, 28
Butch Metzger	48
Roger Metzger	16
Hensley Meulens	31, 37
Jose Mijares	50
Bob Miller	48
Bruce Miller	29
Justin Miller	45
Stu Miller	37
Eddie Milner	12
Damon Minor	22, 37, 1
Greg Minton	41, 42, 38
Stephen Mintz	26
Gino Minutelli	36
Doug Mirabelli	66, 2, 19, 15
Pat Misch	71, 16
Kevin Mitchell	9, 7

Randy Moffitt	39, 17
Dustan Mohr	22
Bengie Molina	1
Bill Monbouquette	39
Carlos Moncrief	39
Johnny Monell	12
Willie Montanez	22
John Montefusco	50, 26
Rich Monteleone	55
Ramon Monzant	41
Bob Moore	31
Matt Moore	45
Jose Morales	28
Joe Morgan	8
Alvin Morman	52
Reyes Moronta	54
Bryan Morris	57
John Morris	42, 43
Matt Morris	35, 22
Michael Morse	38
Guillermo Moscoso	34
Damian Moss	28
Guillermo Mota	59
Manuel Mota	38
Bill Mueller	32
Billy Muffett	36
Terry Mulholland	45, 46
Jack Mull	42
Fran Mullins	16
Scott Munter	54, 47
Masanori Murakami	10, 37
Bobby Murcer	20, 25
Calvin Murray	8
Rich Murray	29

N

Xavier Nady	12, 68
Phil Nastu	14, 25, 23
Joe Nathan	36, 74
Robb Nen	31
Phil Nevin	16
Steve Nicosia	7
Lance Niekro	28
Bob Nieman	20
Donell Nixon	30
Matt Nokes	51
Nick Noonan	21
Bill North	36
Rafael Novoa	36
Eduardo Nunez	10

O

Dan O'Connell	22
Danny O'Connell	19
Billy O'Dell	31
Tom O'Malley	35, 39
Randy O'Neal	55

Ken Oberkfell	10	
Ivan Ochoa	23	
Steven Okert	48, 32	
Francisco Olivares	45	
Al Oliver	0	
Nate Oliver	29	
Steve Ontiveros	16	
John Orsino	34	
Russ Ortiz	60, 48	
Daniel Ortmeier	34, 40	
Josh Osich	61	
Dan Otero	37, 43, 87	
Phil Ouellette	12	
Danny Ozark	3, 1	

P

Angel Pagan	16
Jose Pagan	7, 10, 15
Matt Palmer	50
Joe Panik	12
Jarrett Parker	47, 6
Rick Parker	51, 29, 32
Salty Parker	2
John Patterson	7
Jake Peavy	22, 43
Francisco Peguero	14, 57
Dan Peltier	30
Jim Pena	31
Ramiro Pena	1
Hunter Pence	8
Brad Penny	31
Juan Perez	2
Marty Perez	1
Neifi Perez	1, 10
Tony Perezchica	1, 16, 39
Jon Perlman	46
Ron Perranoski	16
Gaylord Perry	28, 36
Charles "Cap" Peterson	17
Yusmeiro Petit	52
Joe Pettini	2
Dave Philley	32
Dick Phillips	14
J.R. Phillips	31, 13, 17
Mike Phillips	29, 10
Billy Pierce	35, 19
A.J. Pierzynski	36
Joe Pignatano	2
Brett Pill	6
Lee Pitlock	38
Joe Pittman	56
Ed Plank	37
Dick Pole	48
Sidney Ponson	43
Jim Poole	19
Mark Portugal	19

Bill Posedel	1
Buster Posey	28
Alonzo Powell	33
Brian Powell	51
Dante Powell	21, 30, 56
John Pregenzer	40, 18
Joe Price	47
Bob Priddy	38
Ron Pruitt	14, 25
Miguel Puente	41
Brandon Puffer	38
Luis Pujols	55

Q

Luis Quinones	2
Guillermo Quiroz	12, 14
Dan Quisenberry	47

R

John Rabb	31, 5
Dave Rader	6, 14
Gary Rajsich	43
Julio Ramirez	57
Neil Ramirez	59
Ramon Ramirez	52
Cody Ransom	1, 2
Jeff Ransom	3, 16, 37
Pat Rapp	48
Chris Ray	47
Frank Reberger	39
Glenn Redmon	20
Jeff Reed	52
Steve Reed	36, 39
Jessie Reid	26, 31
Ken Reitz	21
Mike Remlinger	14
Marshall Renfroe	21
Edgar Renteria	16
Rick Reuschel	48
Matt Reynolds	57
Dusty Rhodes	26
Frank Riccelli	45
Gene Richards	25
Dave Righetti	19, 46, 32, 33
Bill Rigney	18
Ernest Riles	1
George Riley	28
Armando Rios	1, 36
Allen Ripley	33
Ruben Rivera	21
Joe Roa	37
Dave Roberts	25
Dave Roberts	10
Rich Robertson	48, 43, 45, 49
Craig Robinson	1
Don Robinson	40, 31

Frank Robinson	20
Andre Rodgers	15, 17
Bob Rodgers	8
Felix Rodriguez	47
Guillermo Rodriguez	39
Rich Rodriguez	33
Rick Rodriguez	59
Ron Roenicke	10
Kevin Rogers	21, 28
Ryan Rohlinger	57, 29
Sergio Romo	54
John Roper	42
Jim Rosario	43, 22
Sandy Rosario	43
Don Rose	41
Cody Ross	13
Joe Rosselli	53
Aaron Rowand	33
Mike Rowland	28, 53
Ken Rudolph	6
Kirk Rueter	42, 45, 46
Justin Ruggiano	39
Dan Runzler	37, 45
Josh Rutledge	19

S

Ray Sadecki	37
Mike Sadek	3
Billy Sadler	59, 43
Ryan Sadowski	56
Jeff Samardzija	29
Roger Samuels	58
Alex Sanchez	33, 21
Freddy Sanchez	21
Hector Sanchez	29
Jonathan Sanchez	53, 57
Rey Sanchez	14
Deion Sanders	21
Reggie Sanders	16
Scott Sanderson	21
Pablo Sandoval	48
Jack Sanford	33
Andres Santana	35, 56
F.P. Santangelo	14
Benito Santiago	33
Chad Santos	14
Francisco Santos	60
Mackey Sasser	10, 17
Hank Sauer	6, 27, 7
Steve Scarsone	23
Dan Schatzeder	36
Nate Schierholtz	12
Bob Schmidt	6, 27, 9
Jason Schmidt	29, 22
Dick Schofield	15
Bob Schroder	10, 50

Rick Schu	39
Tim Scott	54
Marco Scutaro	19
Scott Servais	29, 9
Scott Service	34
Adam Shabala	1
Bob Shaw	29
Larry Shepard	8
Pat Sheridan	25
Norm Sherry	34
Tsuyoshi Shinjo	5
Joe Shipley	36, 38, 46, 42
Norm Siebern	7, 29
Dan Slania	57
Austin Slater	53
Reggie Smith	14
Will Smith	13
Duke Snider	28
J.T. Snow	6
Cory Snyder	20
Steve Soderstrom	65
Denny Sommers	58
Lary Sorenson	19
Bill Sorrell	18
Elias Sosa	38
Warren Spahn	21
Denard Span	2
Bob Speake	26
Horace Speed	38
Chris Speier	35, 2
Daryl Spencer	20
Harry Spilman	16
Jerry Spradlin	43, 51
Al Stanek	48
Mike Stanton	38
Herm Starrette	23
James Steels	19
Jeff Stember	50
Rennie Stennett	6
John Stephenson	10, 5
Decker Steve	33
Chris Stewart	37
Steve Stone	33, 29
Joe Strain	20
Chris Stratton	68, 34
Darryl Strawberry	17
Hunter Strickland	60
Drew Stubbs	46
Albert Suarez	56
Andrew Suarez	59
Guy Sularz	21
Champ Summers	6
Eric Surkamp	47
Andrew Susac	34

Russ Swan	33, 52
Mark Sweeney	9
Bill Swift	26

T

John Tamargo	30
Kensuke Tanaka	37
Jack Taschner	37, 48
Stuart Tate	33
Don Taussig	14, 21
Julian Tavarez	52, 50
Bob Taylor	31
Miguel Tejada	10
Ruben Tejada	17
Nick Testa	45, 47
Ryan Theriot	5
Derrel Thomas	30
Valmy Thomas	7
Gary Thomasson	12
Robby Thompson	6, 5
Scot Thompson	41
Erick Threets	60, 48
Mark Thurmond	30
Rusty Tillman	30
Brett Tomko	50, 35
Kelby Tomlinson	37
Tommy Toms	51
Tony Torcato	14, 20, 21
Yorvit Torrealba	9, 8
Andres Torres	59, 56
Salomon Torres	35
Alex Trevino	29
Manny Trillo	9
Michael Tucker	20
Bob Tufts	17

U

Dan Uggla	22
Willie Upshaw	70, 20
Jose Uribe	23
Juan Uribe	5

V

Mike Vail	32
Carlos Valderrama	21
Carlos Valdez	35
Merkin Valdez	37, 47
Sergio Valdez	41
John Van Ornum	42
John Vander Wal	28
William VanLandingham	50
Eugenio Velez	57, 8
Ozzie Virgil	40, 31, 1
Jose Vizcaino	10
Omar Vizquel	13
Ryan Vogelsong	51, 14, 32
Ed Vosberg	28

W

Leon Wagner	39, 48
Kevin Walker	54
Tyler Walker	45, 47
Colin Ward	53
Allen Watson	34, 39
Tony Watson	56
Jim Weaver	45
Ben Weber	57
Todd Wellemeyer	37
Brad Wellman	36
Wes Westrum	9, 3, 6, 38, 5
Steve Whitaker	37
Bill White	23
Eli Whiteside	22, 88
Terry Whitfield	45
Ed Whitson	32
Floyd Wicker	26
Rob Wilfong	9
Rick Wilkins	2
Bernie Williams	20
Charlie Williams	43
Frank Williams	47
Jackson Williams	14
Jerome Williams	57
Keith Williams	42
Matt Williams	10, 9
Mac Williamson	51
Jim Willoughby	19, 42
Brian Wilson	33, 38
Desi Wilson	8, 31
Neil Wilson	6
Trevor Wilson	41, 32
Bobby Winkles	5
Randy Winn	2
Jay Witasick	26
Jim Wohlford	9, 1
Ted Wood	39
Mike Woodard	41
Todd Worrell	45
Al Worthington	32
Ron Wotus	10, 16, 17, 23
Jamey Wright	48

Y

Keiichi Yabu	22
Curt Young	43
Eric Young	21
Joel Youngblood	8

Z

Dom Zanni	45
Chad Zerbe	41
Don Zimmer	1
Barry Zito	75

NY
Christy Mathewson
Pitcher, 1900-1916

NY
John McGraw
Player/Manager, 1902-1906
Manager, 1907-1932

THE NUMBER OF PALM TREES
PLANTED IN WILLIE MAYS PLAZA

THE HEIGHT, IN FEET,
OF THE RIGHT FIELD WALL

THE EXACT WEIGHT, IN POUNDS,
OF THE WORLD SERIES TROPHY

24

THE LUXURY SUITE NUMBER, OUTSIDE OF WHICH HANGS A PHOTOGRAPH
FROM THE FINAL GAME AT CANDLESTICK PARK IN 1999;
WILLIE MAYS IS CAPTURED THROWING OUT THE CEREMONIAL
FIRST PITCH TO HIS GODSON, BARRY BONDS

2½

THE AMOUNT OF HOURS IT TAKES ONE GROUNDSKEEPER TO MOW THE OUTFIELD GRASS

107,000

THE APPROXIMATE SQUARE FOOTAGE OF SOD THAT COVERS THE FIELD

7x7

HE APPROXIMATE SIZE, IN SQUARE MILES, OF THE CITY OF SAN FRANCISCO, AND THE DIMENSIONS, IN INCHES, OF THIS BOOK

ACKNOWLEDGEMENTS

EDITOR
Scott Gummer

PUBLISHER
Peter Gotfredson

DESIGN
Nate Beale/SeeSullivan

CONTRIBUTING WRITER
Kelli Anderson

COPYEDITOR
Mark Nichol

SPECIAL THANKS TO Faham Zakariaei, Valerie McGuire, Nancy Donati, Brian Bisio, Suzanna Mitchell, Bertha Fajardo, Matt Chisholm, Liam Connolly, Doug Kelly, Megan Brown, Katy Batchelder, Matt Valdez, Katja Zimmerman, Donna Bull, Danny Dann, and Mario Alioto.

PHOTOGRAPHY
All photos courtesy of the San Francisco Giants.

www.skyboxpress.com
info@skyboxpress.com
(877) 632-8558

ISBN: 978-1-7320973-1-5

Published by Skybox Press, an imprint of Luxury Custom Publishing, LLC.